THE LITTLE BOOK OF
MERMAIDS

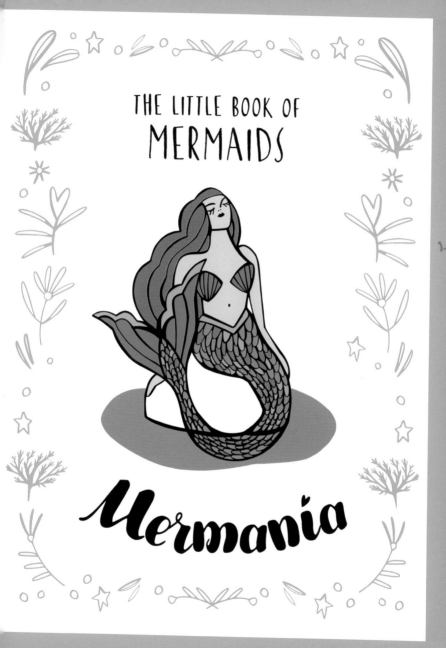

Mermania

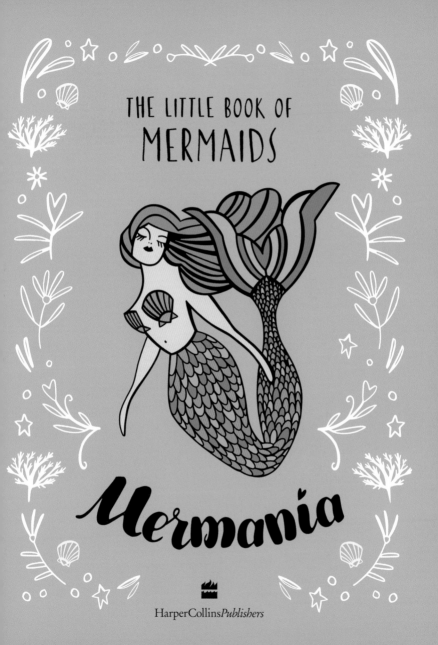

THE LITTLE BOOK OF
MERMAIDS

Mermania

HarperCollins*Publishers*

HarperCollins*Publishers*
1 London Bridge Street
London SE1 9GF

www.harpercollins.co.uk

First published by HarperCollins*Publishers* in 2019

1 3 5 7 9 10 8 6 4 2

Cover and interior illustrations by Laura Korzon
Cover and interior design by Jacqui Caulton
Speech bubble on p. 216 © Shutterstock.com

A catalogue record for this book is
available from the British Library

ISBN: 978-0-00-835801-3

Printed and bound in Latvia

MIX
Paper from
responsible sources
FSC™ C007454

FSC
www.fsc.org

This book is produced from independently certified FSC™ paper
to ensure responsible forest management.

For more information visit: www.harpercollins.co.uk/green

For Wally & Petra –
shapeshifters who always
seem to know who they are

Contents

Always follow your
dreams,
NO MATTER HOW
unrealistic
others think they are.

Introduction

*M*ermaids belong to an enchanted realm. Their seascape is at once tantalizingly out of reach – even the greatest underwater diver must eventually come up for air – and achingly familiar, water being our first home.

From the Middle English word *mere* – meaning lake or sea – mermaids are 'maids of the sea', the stuff of legends, but at the same time ever-present in our modern world. From TV series to music videos, from children's illustrated books to feminist magazines, graffiti, stamps, tattoos, young adult lit, and manga comics, to inspirational postcards and cosy fish-tailed blankets, it seems that wherever you turn, our oceanic alter egos are there. Sprung from ancient fish gods, reborn from the tragedy of forbidden love, combined with the seductive power of the half-bird sirens who sang to Odysseus, and a warning against temptation in the Middle Ages, today mermaids exist as everything from birthday party entertainment to a reclaimed site of political and particularly feminist power.

While we humans dream of being able to breathe underwater – and many a young child longs for the shiny scales of a multi-coloured tail of his or her own – throughout art and story, mermaids are seen yearning for life on land. A 2012 special on the Discovery Channel led viewers to believe that mermaids did in fact exist, a NYC parade near Mermaid Avenue celebrates the dazzling creatures on the Coney Island Boardwalk each year, a bronze statue in Copenhagen has been rebuilt after many attacks by vandals, and from as long ago as the Bronze Age these enchanted creatures have served as our muse.

Surely, part of the mermaid's appeal is how they dramatize our own dilemma – feeling our animal selves to be immortal, something more than the transient beings that we are. Perhaps these magical sea creatures help us to access a place beyond our material existence. And given that most of the world's oceans remain unexplored, how can we be sure they don't really have a material existence themselves?

But perhaps their greatest effect on humans is the way mermaids remake our world. Their desire for a life on land helps us reimagine the one we already have. In their eyes, ordinary elements – air, feet, rain – take on a new hue, becoming extraordinary, even miraculous. Mermaids remind us that the realm to which we belong is enchanted too. Those who love the Earth, with its rising oceans, have increasingly embraced mermaids in their duality – as both harbingers of doom and agents of protection – to swim forward in the fight against climate change.

If mermaids have a legacy that lasts for ages to come, one hopes it will be to help humans preserve the water-filled planet that we're so lucky to have.

Mermaid Names Around the Seven Seas

LATVIA	NARA
IRELAND	MERROW
JAPAN	マーメイド
CARIBBEAN	AYCAYIA
BRAZIL	IARA
RUSSIA AND UKRAINE	RUSALKA
IRAN	پری دریایی
POLAND	SYRENA
DENMARK	HAVFRUE
INUIT MYTHOLOGY	ᓴᓐ
FRANCE	SIRÈNE
CHINA	美人鱼
HAITI	LASIREN
ESTONIA	MERINEITSI

13

History

Throughout history,

mermaids

have been known by many names:

AQUATIC HUMANOID
KELPIE
LIMNIAD
NAIAD
NERIAD
NIX
OCEAN NYMPH

OCEANID
SIREN
SPIRIT
SPRITE
SYLPHE
UNDINE
WATER NYMPH

Mermaids have been
known to live for up to

three hundred
♥ years ♥

in their aquatic form.

TRADING FINS FOR LIFE ON LAND
TENDS TO SHORTEN THEIR LIFESPAN
DRAMATICALLY, PLUS IT OFTEN MEANS

giving up their voices
along with their tails.

IN RETURN, THEY'RE GRANTED A
TERRESTRIAL ROMANCE, OR

perhaps even a soul.

SADLY, IT'S SAID THAT

mermaids

don't have souls;

ONCE THEY DIE THEY SIMPLY

turn into

sea foam.

IN BIBLICAL TERMS
(TO MISQUOTE GENESIS),

For sea foam
thou art, and
unto sea foam
SHALT THOU RETURN.'

19

In the waters off THE PORT OF HISTORIC NYHAVN, IN **Copenhagen,** LIES A WELL-LOVED BRONZE STATUE OF *The Little Mermaid,* MADE BY EDVARD ERIKSEN, WHOSE WIFE POSED FOR THE SCULPTURE.

IN 1909 A BREWER NAMED CARL
JACOBSEN (THE FOUNDER OF CARLSBERG
BEER) COMMISSIONED THE WORK
AFTER FALLING UNDER THE SPELL OF
A BALLET VERSION OF THE FAMOUS
FAIRYTALE. ALTHOUGH MOST GAZE ON
the statue with love
FOR THE QUIET SUNBATHER NEAR THE
LANGELINIE PROMENADE, SHE HAS
SUFFERED VARIOUS ATTACKS. IN 1964 THE
BELOVED STATUE LOST ITS ORIGINAL HEAD.
AN AMPUTATION, ATTEMPTED BEHEADING,
AND EXPLOSION FOLLOWED. SHE HAS BEEN
RESTORED EACH TIME, THOUGH, AND
continues her watch.

Mermaids

CAN SYMBOLIZE ETERNITY, FERTILITY,

beauty, desire, freedom,

mystery, and doom.

Tales about mermaids began to appear

three thousand years ago,

IN THE MESOPOTAMIAN KINGDOM OF ASSYRIA.

MERMAIDS HAVE BEEN ENCHANTING
HUMANS FOR THOUSANDS OF YEARS.
Stories of merfolk
STRETCH BACK THROUGHOUT HISTORY
AND ACROSS CULTURES. IN THE
Babylonian period
(1800–600 BCE), EA, THE GOD OF THE
SEA (IN GREEK, OANNES), HAD THE
*lower body of a fish
and the upper body
of a human.*

26

THE CREATOR OF THE

live mermaid show

AT WEEKI WACHEE SPRINGS, FLORIDA, WAS

'Fish Man' Newton Perry,

A US NAVY VETERAN WHO HAD ONCE
TRAINED NAVY SEALS TO SWIM UNDERWATER
IN WORLD WAR 2. ALTHOUGH THE

city of Weeki Wachee

WAS NOT INCORPORATED UNTIL 1966,
PERRY OPENED THE THEATRE IN OCTOBER
1947. AS OF 2008, THE LEGENDARY
FLORIDA ATTRACTION IS NOW

a state park.

The name
Weeki Wachee
COMES FROM THE SEMINOLE TRIBE
OF NATIVE AMERICANS WHO CALLED
THE SPRING *WEEKIWACHEE*
(winding river).

Explorer Christopher Columbus reported seeing **three mermaids** IN THE OCEAN OFF THE COAST OF WHAT IS NOW THE DOMINICAN REPUBLIC, IN JANUARY 1493. HE SAID THEY 'CAME QUITE HIGH OUT OF THE WATER' BUT WERE 'NOT AS PRETTY AS THEY ARE DEPICTED, for somehow in the face they look like men'.

Moonlight,

CASTING AN ALLURING GLOW ON
AQUATIC MAMMALS, MAY HAVE HELPED
DECEIVE TIRED SEA TRAVELLERS EAGER
FOR A GLIMPSE OF ENCHANTMENT.
MOST REPORTED SIGHTINGS OF

mermaids

*probably mistook
manatees, dugongs,*

AND THE NOW-EXTINCT SEA COWS
FOR THEIR ENCHANTED COUNTERPARTS.
AND AT LEAST ONE CREATIVE EXPLORER
(WILLIAM SCORESBY IN 1820) SAW

*a mermaid figure
in a walrus.*

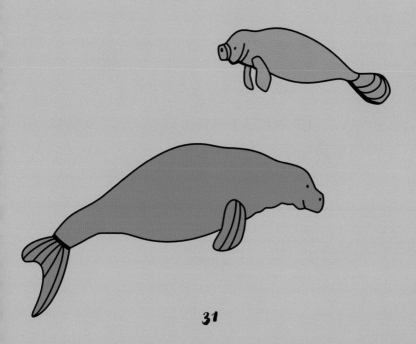

'Dugong'

COMES FROM A MALAY WORD THAT MEANS

'lady of the sea'.

The world's **biggest mermaid**

WAS SAID TO BE 610 METRES (2,000 FEET) *long from head to tail.*

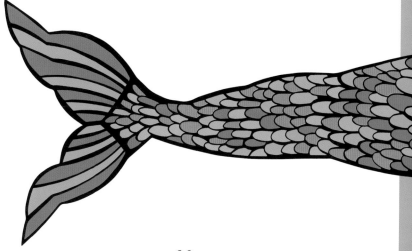

Are mermaids good or bad?

IN SOME STORIES, MERMAIDS APPEAR AS
GENTLE, ROMANTIC FIGURES, ABLE TO
grant wishes, heal,
foretell the future,
AND WARN SAILORS AND FISHERMEN
OF IMMINENT DANGER.

IN OTHER TALES, MERMAIDS ARE

dangerous.

THEY LURE SHIPS TO CRASH ON THE
ROCKS OR USE THEIR SWEET SINGING
VOICES AND RAVISHING LOOKS TO
*tempt men into their
underwater domain*
IN ORDER TO DROWN OR CAPTURE THEM.

IN HIS *NATURAL HISTORY,*
WRITTEN IN THE FIRST CENTURY CE

Pliny the Elder

DOCUMENTED SIGHTINGS OF MERMAIDS
riding upon other
marine creatures.

'AND AS FOR THE MERMAIDS CALLED

Nereides,

IT IS NO FABULOUS TALE THAT GOETH
OF THEM: FOR LOOKE HOW PAINTERS
DRAW THEM, SO THEY ARE INDEED:

only their body is rough
and scaled all over,

EVEN IN THOSE PARTS WHERE THEY
RESEMBLE A WOMAN.'

Gliding silently in boats
made from sealskin,

Inuit whale
hunters

MAY HAVE APPEARED TO BE
HALF SEA CREATURES.

IN HIS *NATURAL HISTORY OF AMBOINA* (1727),

Dutch naturalist

FRANÇOIS VALENTIJN MENTIONED

the capture of a 'monster resembling a siren'.

The combs that **mermaids** HOLD ARE MADE OF FISH BONES.

THE TOP HALF OF A MONKEY SEWN ONTO
A FISH TAIL WAS A POPULAR FEATURE
IN NINETEENTH-CENTURY SIDESHOWS,
DUPING AUDIENCES INTO BELIEVING THEY
WERE SEEING THE REMAINS OF A

real mermaid.

IN 1842, P.T. BARNUM DISPLAYED
ONE SUCH CREATURE — THE SO-CALLED

Fiji mermaid,

WHICH HE CLAIMED TO HAVE BOUGHT
FROM A JAPANESE FISHERMAN — AT HIS
AMERICAN MUSEUM IN NEW YORK CITY.

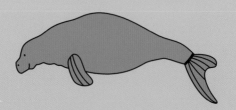

On his second voyage SEARCHING FOR A NORTHWEST PASSAGE ABOVE RUSSIA, SEVENTEENTH-CENTURY **English explorer** Henry Hudson recorded a mermaid sighting on 15 June 1608.

*Here are the notes
from his log book:*

'THIS MORNING ONE OF OUR COMPANIE
LOOKING OVER BOORD SAW A MERMAID
. . . FROM NAVILL UPWARD, HER BACK
AND BREASTS WERE LIKE A WOMAN'S
(AS THEY SAY THAT SAW HER) HER BODY
AS BIG AS ONE OF US; HER SKIN VERY
WHITE; AND LONG HAIRE HANGING DOWN
BEHINDE, OF COLOUR BLACKE; IN HER
GOING DOWNE THEY SAW HER TAYLE, WHICH
WAS LIKE THE TAYLE OF A PORPOSSE AND
SPECKLED LIKE A MACRELL.'

In 1830 a funeral was held to commemorate a

 mermaid

WHOSE DEAD BODY WASHED UP ON THE BEACH AT CULLA BAY ON BENBECULA, ONE OF SCOTLAND'S WESTERN ISLES.

A 1900 account

TRACED HER DEATH TO AN ATTACK AT SGEIR NA DUCHADH A FEW DAYS EARLIER.

It is said her body is buried there near the sea.

LOOK CLOSELY AT THE MAP OF THE

'New World'

FROM 1562, CALLED *THE AMERICAS,
OR A NEW AND PRECISE DESCRIPTION
OF THE FOURTH PART OF THE WORLD.*

Two mermaids

CAN BE SEEN, FLOATING CLOSE TO A SHIP
NEAR THE TIP OF TODAY'S SOUTH AMERICA.

46

'THERE ONCE WAS A VICAR IN BUDE,
WHO DID SOMETHING UNCOMMONLY RUDE.
HE SWAM OUT TO A ROCK,
DONNED SEAWEED FOR LOCKS,
AND SANG WHILE HE BATHED IN THE NUDE.'

True story.

IN THE EARLY NINETEENTH CENTURY,
ROBERT STEPHEN HAWKER OF CORNWALL,
ENGLAND, SWAM OUT TO A ROCK, SANG
IN IMITATION OF A MERMAID FOR THREE
NIGHTS, HIS HEAD DRAPED IN SEAWEED, AND
ATTRACTED QUITE A CROWD. AFTER THE
THIRD NIGHT HE PLUNGED INTO THE WATER
AND WAS NEVER SEEN IN THAT FORM AGAIN.

Are there such things as male mermaids?

INDEED – THEY'RE CALLED

 mermen.

THE GREEK GOD TRITON, FOR EXAMPLE, LOOKS LIKE WHAT YOU MIGHT IMAGINE A MERMAN TO BE. ON THE OTHER HAND, THE MALE MERROW COOMARA ('SEA-HOUND') HAS GREEN TEETH AND SCALY LEGS.

49

Take a look at your cup the next time you're at Starbucks.

YOU'LL SEE THE WOMAN IN

the logo

is a two-tailed mermaid, THOUGH THE GRAPHIC HAS CHANGED CONSIDERABLY SINCE 1971 WHEN IT FIRST APPEARED AND SHOWED A LOT MORE SKIN (AND SCALES).

The company's name came before its logo.

STARBUCKS CAME FROM MR STARBUCK, FIRST MATE OF THE *PEQUOD* IN HERMAN MELVILLE'S CLASSIC *MOBY-DICK*. TO CONTINUE THE MARITIME THEME, ADVERTISING CONSULTANT TERRY HECKLER CREATED THE ICONIC MERMAID

logo we know today.

IF TOURING CORNWALL (FOR ITS MERMAID LORE, IF FOR NO OTHER REASON), YOU'LL WANT TO AVOID THE

Doom Bar

WHERE THE RIVER CAMEL MEETS THE SEA. LOCAL LEGEND ATTRIBUTES ITS CREATION TO A MERMAID'S REVENGE FOR HER DEATH AT THE HANDS OF A SAILOR. TRUE OR NOT, MANY A SHIP HAS BEEN DESTROYED ON THIS SANDBANK.

IN JAPANESE FOLKLORE,
eating Ningyo
(mermaids)
IS SAID TO GRANT LONGEVITY.

'The water spirits were known under such names as oreades, nereides, limoniades, naiades, water sprites, sea maids, mermaids, and potamides. Often the water nymphs derived their names from the streams, lakes, or seas in which they dwelt.'

— *THE SECRET TEACHINGS OF ALL AGES*,
MANLY P. HALL (1928)

IN 2009, SEVERAL

*independent reports of
mermaid sightings*

IN THE SMALL TOWN OF KIRYAT YAM,
ON THE MEDITERRANEAN COAST OF
ISRAEL, LED TO AN OFFER OF

 $1 million

FOR THE LUCKY PHOTOGRAPHER WHO MANAGED
TO CAPTURE THE CREATURE ON FILM.

*So far the reward has
gone unclaimed.*

WANTED

HAVE YOU SEEN THIS MERMAID?

$1 MILLION REWARD

KNOWN ASSOCIATES: SEAHORSES, SEALS, & MANATEES

LAST SIGHTED LOUNGING ON A ROCK

Mythology

*M*any who grew up enchanted by Ariel from Disney's *The Little Mermaid* are surprised to find how dark and even gruesome the Hans Christian Andersen version of the story is. Those who dive deeper into the history and mythology of mermaids will find many elements they recognize in the Danish author's fairytale. Many mermaid stories are tales of suffering and woe, betrayal, and revenge, often ending unhappily ever after, with many an abandoned family. Still, there are cultures that celebrate mermaids as symbolizing good luck, and the themes of rebirth and second chances run across cultures.

A multiplicity of meanings and traditions has grown out of different cultures coming into contact with each other and interweaving their beliefs. More surprising than the variety is the universal quality of the polymorphic figure – the fact that so many half-woman half-fish stories seem to have emerged independently.

The modern version imagines mermaids who want a chance at life, but in myths the mermaid incarnation is often a drowned woman given a second chance.

The waters around Ireland were once home to Liban, a half-salmon woman who had survived the flood that killed her family by transforming into a mermaid. Captured after a long underwater life, she was given the name Muirgen ('sea-born') and ascended to heaven.

Fish women

IN EARLY MESOPOTAMIAN ART WERE CALLED *KULITU*.

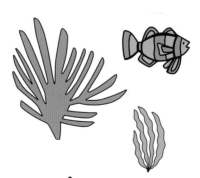

IN SCOTLAND, BEAUTIFUL
WOMEN KNOWN AS

Selkies

turn into seals when
they enter water.

ON LAND, THEY SHED THEIR SEAL
SKIN, BUT THEY'LL NEVER BE ABLE
TO RETURN TO THE SEA WITHOUT IT.
SOME LEGENDS SAY THE

'Seal Fairies' emerge
on Midsummer Eve.

63

THE AFRICAN WATER SPIRIT,

Mami Wata

(MUMMY WATER), IS OFTEN DEPICTED WITH
A SNAKE OR CROCODILE ADDED TO HER
FISH-WOMAN BODY. SHE IS A HEALER BUT
CONTAINS AN ELEMENT OF DANGER, LIKE
OTHERS IN THE WATER SPIRIT TRADITION.

*She's said to like
shiny baubles.*

ENSLAVEMENT AND TRANSPORT OF
AFRICANS AT THE HANDS OF EUROPEAN
COLONIZERS LED TO A SHARED TRADITION
ACROSS THE SEA WHERE, IN THE
CARIBBEAN, FOR EXAMPLE, LA SIRÈNE
CLOSELY RESEMBLES MAMI WATA.

BEFORE THE FAMILIAR HALF-HUMAN HALF-FISH IMAGERY CAME INTO POPULARITY, *water gods* WERE SHOWN DRESSED IN THE *skins of fish.*

In the Gocta waterfall
in Peru,
A MERMAID, A FISHERMAN, AND HIS
WIFE FOUND THEMSELVES IN AN
UNFORTUNATE LOVE TRIANGLE WHEN
THE MERMAID NOT ONLY BOOSTED
the fisherman's catch
but added a little
bit of gold, too.

ON THE RIVERBANKS OF RUSSIA,
STRANGE CREATURES CALLED

*Rusalki emerge from
the water at night*

TO SING AND DANCE, BUT THE FESTIVE
APPEARANCE OBSCURES THE REASON FOR
THEIR PRESENCE. IN THEIR LAND LIVES,
THESE WOMEN DIED VIOLENTLY, SOME OF
THEM DROWNED. TO AVENGE THEIR DEATHS,
THE MERMAID-LIKE CREATURES SING AND
DANCE, HOPING TO SEDUCE OTHERS
AND LURE THEM TO THE SAME FATE.

67

In Inuit mythology,

MANY VERSIONS OF THE STORY OF THE SEA GODDESS

Sedna

ARE TOLD. IN ONE, SEDNA DOESN'T WANT TO MARRY ANY OF THE HUNTERS THAT HER FATHER CHOOSES FOR HER. TRICKED INTO MARRYING ONE WHO TURNS OUT TO BE A BIRD, SHE ATTEMPTS TO ESCAPE WITH THE HELP OF HER FATHER.

BUT THE BIRD SUMMONS A FIERCE
STORM AND SEDNA'S FATHER
MUST THROW HIS DAUGHTER INTO
THE SEA TO SAVE HER FROM IT.

*She survives in a new
form as a mermaid.*

IN ANOTHER VERSION OF THE STORY,
SEDNA'S FATHER HURLS HER INTO THE SEA
AFTER SHE ATTACKS HIM. SHE ATTEMPTS
TO CLING ON TO THE KAYAK, BUT HE CUTS
HER FINGERS. THEY ARE REBORN WITH HER,

as creatures of the sea.

FROM THE LATE FRENCH MEDIEVAL
PERIOD COMES THE HAUNTING STORY
OF A MAIDEN WITH A SCALY SECRET.

The beautiful Melusine

HAS A PAST SHE DOESN'T WANT TO SHARE.
ON SATURDAYS, WHEN SHE BATHES, SHE
TAKES HER TRUE HALF-FISH (OR SOMETIMES
SERPENT) FORM, A KIND OF 'BIRTHDAY
SUIT' THAT COULD BE A BIT ALARMING
FOR THE UNINITIATED. MELUSINE WISELY
ASKS FOR PRIVACY FROM HER HUSBAND
FOR THIS WEEKLY RITUAL, BUT WHEN
HER CURIOUS LOVER CATCHES SIGHT
OF HER INNER SERPENT, SHE IMMEDIATELY

flees for her life.

70

71

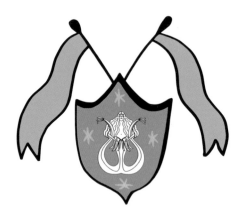

MELUSINE'S TAIL DOESN'T TROUBLE
THE MANY NOBLE EUROPEAN FAMILIES
WHO CLAIM HER FOR THEIR ANCESTOR,
DEPICTING HER IN THEIR

coat of arms

AND PROUDLY EMBRACING THEIR
mermaid heritage.

Warsaw,

IN POLAND, MAY BE NAMED AFTER THE
ORIGINAL CELEBRITY COUPLE NICKNAME.
Wars, a fisherman,
IS SAID TO HAVE RESCUED
A CAPTIVE MERMAID
named Sawa.

THE JAPANESE
mermaid,
the Ningyo,
HAS THE MOUTH OF A MONKEY.

THE NATIVE AMERICAN PASSAMAQUODDY
TRIBE TELL A TALE OF TWO DEFIANT
SKINNY-DIPPING GIRLS WHO GREW
*fish tails after too much
time spent underwater.*

Humans aren't the only ones who get to be half fish.

Hippocampi

(GROWN-UP SEAHORSES) WERE
MARINE HORSES WITH FISH TAILS

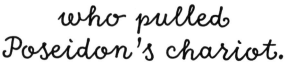

who pulled
Poseidon's chariot.

ON 6 APRIL EVERY YEAR, INDONESIAN FISHERMEN IN THE TOWN OF PELABUHAN RATU, IN WEST JAVA, CELEBRATE THE MERMAID GODDESS NYAI LORO KIDUL –

the 'Queen of the Southern Sea' –

PRAYING FOR HER BLESSING AND SENDING OFFERINGS INTO THE SEA.

ONE OF THE ORIGINAL MERMAID
*myths is a tale of
star-crossed love.*

The goddess of the moon and water,

ATARGATIS, FELL IN LOVE WITH
A MORTAL SHEPHERD CALLED HADAD.
THOUGH THEY HAD A DAUGHTER WHO
LATER BECAME THE QUEEN OF ASSYRIA,

Atargatis accidentally killed her forbidden lover, Hadad.

IN GUILT AND TORMENT, SHE THREW HERSELF INTO A LAKE WHERE SHE WAS transformed into a mermaid.

Atargatis

FROM ASSYRIAN MYTH LATER turned into Derketo IN GREEK MYTHOLOGY AND Dea Syria in Roman.

THERE ONCE WAS A YOUNG MERMAID,

Suvannamaccha,

the golden mermaid of Thailand.

WHEN HER DEMON FATHER ASKED FOR HER HELP THWARTING AN ENEMY, SHE HAD NO CHOICE BUT TO OBEY. HER FATHER WAS HOLDING THE BEAUTIFUL SITA, WIFE OF LORD RAMA, CAPTIVE ON THE ISLAND OF LANKA. THE HINDU MONKEY GOD HANUMAN WAS TRYING TO BUILD A BRIDGE OF ROCKS TO RESCUE SITA. EACH DAY, HANUMAN LAID DOWN AS MANY HEAVY ROCKS AS HE COULD AND EACH DAY THE GOLDEN MERMAID AND HER FRIENDS REMOVED JUST AS MANY TO A CAVE FAR AWAY.

BUT WHEN HANUMAN AND SUVANNAMACCHA
FELL IN LOVE, THE MERMAID CHANGED HER
MIND AND DECIDED TO HELP REBUILD
the bridge she'd spent so
much time destroying.
IN THE END, SHE HAD TO TAKE LEAVE OF
HER LOVE, EVEN AS SHE CARRIED HIS SON.

IT IS SAID THAT FOR CENTURIES AFTER HE DIED, *Alexander the Great's sister Thessalonike* HAUNTED THE AEGEAN SEA. WHEN SHIPS PASSED, SHE ASKED FOR NEWS OF HER BROTHER. SHE WANTED TO HEAR ONLY ONE THING – THAT ALEXANDER LIVED AND CONTINUED HIS REIGN. SAILORS GIVING THIS REPORT WERE SENT HAPPILY ON THEIR WAY. THOSE WHO DID NOT BRING GOOD TIDINGS FACED THE WRATH OF THESSALONIKE, WHO TRANSFORMED INTO *a Gorgon and destroyed the ships.*

83

A four-footed

MERMAID IS MENTIONED IN THE
ancient Chinese text
SHAN HAI JING, BELIEVED TO BE FROM THE
FOURTH CENTURY BCE, IF NOT EARLIER.

SHAN HAI JING

NATURAL HISTORY OF THE WORLD

MOBY-DICK

HOMER *The Odyssey*

Freshwater mermaids
WHO LIVE IN ARNHEM LAND, IN
NORTHWEST AUSTRALIA, ARE CALLED

 Yawk Yawks.

LISTEN CLOSELY TO THE SOUND OF THE
WATERFALL THERE – IN IT YOU WILL HEAR
the mermaids' voices.

Science

Research into the symbology and mythology of mermaids could be a life's work, but there is a science to this book as well. After all, we must figure out how mermaids breed, how they breathe, and how we can protect their habitat. For many centuries, mermaid-related inquiries were pursued as part of natural history, eventually passing into the more spurious realm of curiosities. More recently, Professor Karl Banse at the University of Washington wrote a peculiar article called 'Mermaids – Their Biology, Culture, and Demise'. One guesses the article is meant to be satirical, while still offering valuable information about one of the world's longest, cross-cultural topics of inquiry. Despite our 3,000-plus-year obsession with mermaids, at present scientists estimate the oceans remain 95 per cent unexplored. When it comes to these interspecies creatures, much is left to discover.

In Professor Banse's article, the oceanographer argued that the fish-tailed women were a legitimate area of inquiry and tied their demise to surging jellyfish populations due to an oceanic imbalance caused by overfishing.

How are mermaids born?

ALTHOUGH IN ONE FOLK STORY

a merbaby was born through the throat,

IN MOST CASES, AS FOR UNICORNS,
NO ONE SEEMS TO KNOW.

Monstrorum
Historia

THE COLLECTION OF WOODCUT
ILLUSTRATIONS IN *MONSTRORUM HISTORIA*,
by sixteenth-century
Italian naturalist
ULISSE ALDROVANDI, DOCUMENTED BOTH
REAL HUMAN ABNORMALITIES AND THOSE
OF MYTHOLOGICAL CREATURES. IT FEATURED
A HIDEOUS MERMAID COUPLE WITH
webbed feet coming out
of their tails and with
horns on their heads.
(RELATED ENTRIES INCLUDE A SEA MONK
AND SEA BISHOP.)

MADII PAGE IS A WIRADJURI
(INDIGENOUS AUSTRALIAN ABORIGINAL)

'*mermaid*'

WHO DRAWS ON HER NATIVE UNDERSTANDING
OF THE COASTAL CLIMATE TO ADVOCATE FOR
protecting the ocean and
fighting climate change.

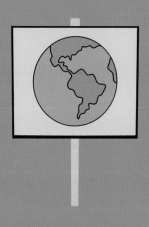

MANY MERMAID-LOVERS LEND THEIR
VOICES TO THE FIGHT FOR

marine conservation,

EDUCATING THE PUBLIC ABOUT THE

hazards of
plastic bottles,

FOR EXAMPLE, MOST OF WHICH GO
UNRECYCLED AND MANY OF WHICH
END UP IN THE SEA.

The Angry Mermaid Award

WAS GIVEN OUT IN 2009 TO AGROCHEMICAL COMPANY MONSANTO IN ADVANCE OF THE COPENHAGEN CLIMATE TALKS. VOTERS CHOSE THE 'WINNER' BASED ON *which company did the most* **damage** TO ENVIRONMENTAL EFFORTS.

FRESHLY SQUEEZED
MERMAID
TEARS
NOT FROM CONCENTRATE

GIVEN THE MANY WAYS IN WHICH HUMANS
HAVE POLLUTED THE OCEANS, AND IN THE
PROCESS DISRUPTED ECOSYSTEMS, INCLUDING
FOOD SOURCES FOR ALL MARINE CREATURES,

mermaids

– IF THEY EXIST – WOULD LIKELY BE AN
ENDANGERED SPECIES. SUSTAINABILITY
CONSULTANT SUSETTE HORSPOOL
SPECULATES THAT SURVIVING MERMAIDS
COULD POSSIBLY HAVE FOUND A HOME NEAR
hydrothermal vents –

OPENINGS ALONG THE SEA FLOOR
WHERE WATER IS HEATED BY MAGMA.
SOMEWHAT COINCIDENTALLY,
THE DEEP-SEA CARTILAGINOUS
fish known as skate
HAVE BEEN KNOWN TO INCUBATE THEIR
EGGS ALONG HYDROTHERMAL VENTS IN
A PROTECTIVE COVERING CALLED A
'mermaid's purse'
(shown below).

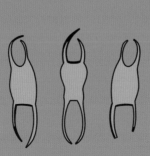

IN 1979,

oceanographer

Sylvia Earle,

AKA 'HER DEEPNESS', BECAME A
MERMAID OF SORTS, WHEN SHE
WALKED ON THE OCEAN FLOOR FOR
two and a half hours.

LEGENDARY ITALIAN RENAISSANCE
ARTIST AND INVENTOR

Leonardo da Vinci

WOULD LIKELY HAVE BEEN IMPRESSED
WITH THE BREATHING HOSE USED
BY WEEKI WACHEE MERMAIDS.
*The underwater
breathing apparatus*
THAT DA VINCI SKETCHED IN HIS *CODEX
ATLANTICUS* IN 1500 WAS EVENTUALLY
MADE UP INTO A DESIGN THAT IS NOW MORE
COMMONLY KNOWN AS SCUBA-DIVING GEAR.

NEIL SHUBIN,
*evolutionary biologist
and author of*
YOUR INNER FISH, THINKS

 biccups

RESULT FROM A BREATHING
MECHANISM RELATED TO OUR
aquatic past.

WONDERING WHAT KIND OF FISH ARE
related to mermaids?

Pelagic fish,

ACCORDING TO GEORGE PARSONS,
DIRECTOR OF FISHES AT THE SHEDD
AQUARIUM IN CHICAGO.

MERMAIDS
THE BODY FOUND

Viewers were tricked
BY ANIMAL PLANET'S 2012 SPECIAL,
MERMAIDS: THE BODY FOUND, INTO
BELIEVING THEY WERE WATCHING A
DOCUMENTARY ABOUT EVIDENCE THAT
MERMAIDS DID EXIST. IN RESPONSE, THE
NATIONAL OCEANIC AND ATMOSPHERIC
ADMINISTRATION PUT OUT AN OFFICIAL
STATEMENT RESPONDING TO THE QUESTION:

'Are mermaids real?'

Here is what they wrote:

'NO EVIDENCE OF AQUATIC HUMANOIDS HAS EVER BEEN FOUND. WHY, THEN, DO THEY OCCUPY THE COLLECTIVE UNCONSCIOUS OF NEARLY ALL SEAFARING PEOPLES? THAT'S A QUESTION BEST LEFT TO HISTORIANS, PHILOSOPHERS, AND ANTHROPOLOGISTS.'

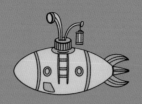

UNDETERRED BY THE
vast misunderstanding
(OR PERHAPS SPURRED ON BY IT),
A YEAR LATER ANIMAL PLANET
released a follow-up
mockumentary:
MERMAIDS: THE NEW EVIDENCE.

A COMMON CASE OF MISTAKEN IDENTITY
(SEE P. 30) GAVE RISE TO THE NAME

Sirenia

FOR THE TAXONOMIC ORDER OF AQUATIC
MAMMALS THAT INCLUDES DUGONGS AND
MANATEES. ALTHOUGH HOMER'S SIRENS
WERE RATHER UNAPPEALING HALF-BIRD
WOMEN (SEE P. 141), THEIR SEDUCTIVE
QUALITIES MERGED WITH THE HALF-FISH
MERMAID FORM TO CREATE THE ENCHANTING
SIREN MERMAID WE KNOW TODAY.

'...now the materialism of the present age would shatter, if it could, our cherished belief in these Marine eccentricities'.

— JOHN ASHTON, NINETEENTH-CENTURY NATURALIST

Neptune's

THIRD-BIGGEST MOON,
NEREID, IS NAMED FOR THE

saltwater nymph

OF GREEK MYTHOLOGY (NOT TO BE
CONFUSED WITH THE *FRESHWATER* NYMPH
KNOWN AS THE NAIAD). ALTHOUGH BOTH
OF THESE MERMAID-RELATED SPIRITS
ARE SOMETIMES DEPICTED WITH TAILS,
TYPICALLY THEY'RE IMAGINED AS MORE
TRADITIONAL (IF SUPERNATURAL)

female figures.

Some say
mermaids

HAVE GILLS ON THE SIDE OF THEIR NECK;
OTHERS SAY THEY CAN'T ACTUALLY
BREATHE UNDERWATER, BUT SIMPLY

*hold their breath for
a really long time.*

In the sixteenth century, A DOCTOR IN A PORTUGUESE COLONY IN INDIA DISSECTED A CAPTIVE MERMAID; COMPARED TO THEIR LAND COUNTERPARTS, no major differences were found.

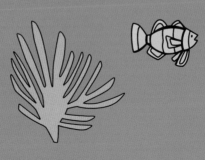

The single-celled

algae plant

ACETABULARIA ACETABULUM IS KNOWN
TO MOST CASUAL OBSERVERS AS THE
'MERMAID'S WINE GLASS'. THE LOVELY
PLANT AND ITS NAME ARE THE STUFF
OF MARINE BOTANISTS' DAYDREAMS,
BUT NEW RESEARCH SUGGESTS
INCREASED OCEANIC ACIDIFICATION
HAS WEAKENED THE PLANT,
possibly changing both
its shape and colour.

109

Art, Literature & Popular Culture

These changeable figures have shapeshifted their way across the world, from Japan to Peru, from Arctic waters to the Mexican desert (yes, at least one mermaid exists on dry land). They've plunged their way into opera and ballets, swum along with parades, found themselves captive in romantic poetry, the muse of Victorian painters, and the inspiration for countless childrens' tales. Today you can even go to an academy to learn to be one yourself.

Aphrodite,
goddess of love,

BORN OF SEA FOAM, WAS DELIVERED TO THE
SHORE IN A SCALLOP SHELL. SURELY SHE
OWES A DEBT TO HER MERMAID ANCESTORS?
LOOK CLOSELY AT SANDRO BOTTICELLI'S
1485 PAINTING *THE BIRTH OF VENUS*.
YOU'LL NOTICE THE FEET ARE PAINTED
IN A SHAPE THAT RESEMBLES A FIN.

Long before Ron Howard's 1984 mermaid film bit

MADE A *Splash* ACROSS CINEMA SCREENS EVERYWHERE, A BRITISH COMEDY ENTERTAINED VIEWERS – THE 1948 FILM *MIRANDA*. ON HOLIDAY ALONG THE COAST OF CORNWALL, A DOCTOR MEETS A MERMAID WHO TRAPS HIM INTO BRINGING HER TO LONDON. (CURIOUS ABOUT BABY MERFOLK? LOOK FOR THE SCENE WITH MIRANDA'S MERBABY AT THE MOVIE'S END.)

'Part of Your World',
SUNG BY ARIEL IN THE 1989 DISNEY
animated film
THE LITTLE MERMAID,
HAS BEEN EMBRACED BY MANY IN
THE LGBTQ COMMUNITY, WHO RELATE
TO THE REJECTION OF TRADITION
AND A LONGING FOR A COLOURFUL,
unattainable world.
(THE PART OF URSULA THE SEA WITCH,
WHO CONVINCES ARIEL TO GIVE UP HER
VOICE FOR A LIFE ABOVE WATER, WAS
INSPIRED BY THE DRAG QUEEN AND JOHN
WATERS' STAR DIVINE, PLAYED BY THE
ACTOR HARRIS GLENN MILSTEAD.)

117

High couture ISN'T JUST FOR WOMEN ANY MORE. ERIC DUCHARME, AKA THE **'Mertailor',** DESIGNS ALL KINDS OF FANCY FANTASY SWIMWEAR FOR BOTH MEN AND WOMEN. *Moon Kelp Whimsy and Ocean Spray Whimsy* ARE TWO OF HIS REALISTIC-LOOKING PRODUCTS. INSPIRED AS A CHILD BY FREQUENT VISITS TO SEE LIVE MERMAID SHOWS AT WEEKI WACHEE SPRINGS (SEE P. 27), DUCHARME WAS TAUGHT TO SEW AT THE AGE OF EIGHT BY HIS GRANDMOTHER.

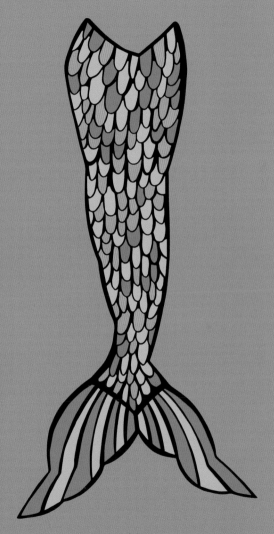

119

In Zennor chapel

IN CORNWALL, A CARVING FROM THE FIFTEENTH CENTURY KNOWN AS

the 'mermaid chair'

SHOWS A HALF-FISH HALF-WOMAN CREATURE HOLDING A MIRROR AND A COMB. MERMAID CARVINGS WERE POPULAR IN EUROPEAN CHURCHES IN THE MIDDLE AGES, PLACED TO WARN WOULD-BE SINNERS AGAINST *temptations of the flesh.*

In the classic
American novel

MOBY-DICK BY HERMAN MELVILLE,
SOME OF THE SAILORS ON THE
PEQUOD THINK THEY HEAR THE SOUND
OF MERMAIDS. OTHERS ATTRIBUTE
THE INHUMAN SOUND TO 'NEWLY
DROWNED MEN'.

'AT LAST, WHEN THE SHIP DREW NEAR
TO THE OUTSKIRTS, AS IT WERE, OF THE
EQUATORIAL FISHING-GROUND, AND IN THE
DEEP DARKNESS THAT GOES BEFORE THE
DAWN, WAS SAILING BY A CLUSTER OF ROCKY
ISLETS; THE WATCH – THEN HEADED BY FLASK
– WAS STARTLED BY A CRY SO PLAINTIVELY
WILD AND UNEARTHLY – LIKE HALF-
ARTICULATED WAILINGS OF THE GHOSTS OF
ALL HEROD'S MURDERED INNOCENTS...'

– HERMAN MELVILLE, *MOBY-DICK*

The original pitch

FOR THE 1984 ROM-COM

Splash

WAS FROM THE MERMAID'S POINT OF VIEW. SCREENWRITER BRIAN GRAZER'S IDEA WAS REJECTED HUNDREDS OF TIMES BEFORE HE FLIPPED THE SCRIPT TO SUGGEST A LOVE STORY FROM THE MAN'S PERSPECTIVE. (THE FAMOUS ORANGE FIN THAT DARYL HANNAH ACTUALLY WORE – INSPIRED BY KOI AND GOLDFISH – weighed 16kg (35 pounds).)

HOLLYWOOD RUMOUR HAS IT THAT DARYL HANNAH LIKED TO SWIM AROUND *'mermaid style'* AS A CHILD, WHICH MAY HAVE HELPED HER LAND THE ROLE OF MADISON IN THE HIT FILM.

The Mermaid Stretch

IN YOGA, CALLED NAGINYASANA IN
SANSKRIT, IS A VARIATION ON THE

pigeon pose.

WITH ONE LEG BENT ON THE FLOOR IN
FRONT AND THE OTHER BEHIND, BENT
UPWARDS AT THE KNEE, THE GOAL IS TO
HOLD THE BACK LEG UP WITH THE ELBOW
WHILE ONE'S HANDS ARE OVERHEAD,
CLASPED TOGETHER IN A DIAMOND SHAPE.
THOUGH IT SOUNDS RATHER INELEGANT,
THE EFFECT IS QUITE GRACEFUL. (PLEASE
ONLY ATTEMPT WITH EXPERT GUIDANCE.)

Harry Potter fans
WILL BE FAMILIAR WITH THE SPOOKY

merpeople

WHO FIRST APPEAR IN *HARRY POTTER AND THE GOBLET OF FIRE* AND LIVE UNDERWATER IN THE GREAT LAKE AT HOGWARTS, SPEAKING MERMISH. IN A TWIST ON THE USUAL MYTH, THEIR MELODIOUS SEA SONGS DID NOT TRANSLATE ABOVE WATER. (HARRY, HOWEVER, ADAPTS WELL TO THE AQUATIC ENVIRONMENT, GROWING GILLS AND WEBBED FEET.)

127

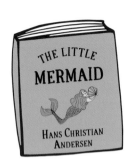

Watching his friend
EDVARD COLLIN MARRY A WOMAN
TORMENTED AUTHOR

Hans Christian Andersen.

IT WAS THIS HEARTBREAK THAT
PROPELLED HIM INTO WRITING THE
IMMORTAL TALE OF IMPOSSIBLE LOVE
WE KNOW AS *THE LITTLE MERMAID*.

Stage actress
Jodi Benson

HAD TO WORK TO TURN HER POWERFUL SINGING VOICE (AKA HER BROADWAY BELT) INTO THE *gentle voice of Ariel* IN DISNEY'S *THE LITTLE MERMAID*.

The mermaid who was featured in the 1483 **Nuremberg Bible** HAD TIME TO LOOK INTO HER MIRROR, AS HER MERDOG AND A MERMAN SWAM NEARBY, apparently untroubled by Noah's flood.

In his surrealist 1934 painting

Collective Invention,

BELGIAN ARTIST RENÉ MAGRITTE REVERSES THE TYPICAL HALF-FISH HALF-WOMAN MERMAID. IN HIS VERSION THE FISH HALF IS ON TOP AND THE FEMALE HALF ON THE BOTTOM. THE FIGURE IS LYING ON THE BEACH ALONG THE SHORELINE, ON HER SIDE FACING FRONT, LOOKING A BIT TRAPPED. IT APPEARS SHE COULD WALK QUITE EASILY ON LAND, BUT IT'S UNCLEAR HOW WELL SHE CAN BREATHE.

THE MERMAID'S VOICE WAS

fully weaponized

IN A JAPANESE SHŌJO MANGA SERIES 'MERMAID MELODY PICHI PICHI PITCH' THAT WAS CREATED BY MICHIKO YOKOTE IN THE EARLY 2000S. INSTEAD OF SEDUCING, HERE A MERMAID SONG HELPS *Princess Lucia Nanami repel the sea demon.*

A lighthouse keeper

ISN'T AN OCCUPATION WHERE YOU
EXPECT TO MEET MANY POTENTIAL MATES.
PERHAPS IT'S NOT SO SURPRISING
THEN THAT ONE KEEPER

fell in love with
a mermaid,

WHO THEN GAVE BIRTH TO THEIR DAUGHTER,
WHO TELLS THE TALE OF HER STRANGE
ORIGIN IN THE EIGHTEENTH-CENTURY SEA
SHANTY 'THE KEEPER OF THE EDDYSTONE',
LATER COVERED AS 'THE EDDYSTONE LIGHT'.

'More scientists than sirens, the mermaids gather specimens with the stalking skill of anglerfish'.

— 'THE NATURALIST'S DREAM OF MERMAIDS COLLECTING IN THE DEEP', KEELY SARR

134

Want to become
a mermaid yourself
(or perhaps a Triton)?

IF YOU'RE NOT YET READY TO
DIVE INTO WEEKI WACHEE SPRINGS
(SEE P. 27), PERHAPS YOU'D LIKE TO
VISIT THE SIRENAS MEDITERRANEAN
ACADEMY NEAR BARCELONA, SPAIN, AND
start working on your
tail techniques.

THOUGH WEARING ONE GOT HER
ARRESTED IN 1907, WE HAVE

'the original mermaid'

ANNETTE KELLERMANN TO THANK FOR
ONE-PIECE FEMALE BATHING SUITS INSTEAD
OF THE HEAVY WOOL, DRESS-BLOOMER
NUMBERS THAT WOMEN WORE UP UNTIL
THAT POINT. THE AUSTRALIAN SWIMMER AND
ACTRESS STARRED IN MANY A MERMAID-
INSPIRED MOVIE, INCLUDING *SIREN OF
THE SEA*, *THE MERMAID*, AND *NEPTUNE'S
DAUGHTER*. (SHE ALSO PERFORMED HER OWN
STUNTS AND ONCE DIVED INTO A PIT OF
CROCODILES FOR A ROLE.)

Some mermaids are bloodthirsty, some merely... absent-minded.

IN HIS 1909 POEM 'THE MERMAID' IRISH POET

William Butler Yeats

MEMORIALIZED ONE OF THE LATTER:

'A MERMAID FOUND A SWIMMING LAD,
PICKED HIM FOR HER OWN,
PRESSED HER BODY TO HIS BODY,
LAUGHED; AND PLUNGING DOWN
FORGOT IN CRUEL HAPPINESS
THAT EVEN LOVERS DROWN.'

In the painted picture book

JULIÁN IS A MERMAID (2019), BY NEW YORK CITY ACTRESS JESSICA LOVE, JULIÁN IS WORRIED ABOUT HOW HIS *ABUELA* (GRANDMA) WILL REACT TO

his love of mermaids.

HE FINDS OUT WHEN SHE BRINGS HIM TO THE ANNUAL CONEY ISLAND MERMAID PARADE!

BEFORE KATY PERRY, LADY GAGA,
OR EVEN MADONNA TOOK THEIR
INSPIRATION FROM THEIR SEA SISTERS,

German composer
Felix Mendelssohn

COMPOSED *THE FAIR MELUSINE* (1834) TO
THE DOOMED ENCHANTRESS OF MERMAID
MYTH. (MENDELSSOHN IS BEST KNOWN
FOR HIS 'WEDDING MARCH.')

'This is where the merfolk lived long ago, ruled over by the Sea King. His castle lay in the deepest part of the ocean and was made of seashells and mother-of-pearl that gleamed in the dappled half-light.'

— *THE LITTLE MERMAID*, RETOLD BY AUTHOR AND ILLUSTRATOR JANE RAY

THE FAMED SWEET-VOICED
sirens of Homer's
Odyssey
WERE NOT MERMAIDS, AS THEY'VE COME TO BE IMAGINED, BUT RATHER HALF-BIRD HALF-WOMAN CREATURES. EMILY WILSON, THE FIRST FEMALE TRANSLATOR INTO ENGLISH OF HOMER'S 3,000-YEAR-OLD EPIC, SAYS

they were alluring because of their knowledge, not their physical appeal.

When little Saoirse
FINDS HER VOICE AT THE END OF
THE 2014 HAND-DRAWN,

animated film

SONG OF THE SEA (IN IRISH,
AMHRÁN NA MARA), SHE DISCOVERS
THE SECRET OF HER BIRTH
(HER MOTHER IS A SELKIE) AND

seals gather round
to listen to her
beautiful song.

ALTHOUGH WHEN IT COMES TO MERMAIDS

William Shakespeare

IS PERHAPS BEST KNOWN FOR OBERON REMINDING PUCK ABOUT ONCE HEARING A MERMAID'S SONG IN *A MIDSUMMER NIGHT'S DREAM*, OR ANTIPHOLUS CALLING LUCIANA A MERMAID IN *THE COMEDY OF ERRORS*, IN THE HISTORY PLAY *HENRY VI*, RICHARD III GIVES A CHILLING SOLILOQUY PROMISING TO 'DROWN MORE SAILORS THAN THE MERMAID SHALL'.

AND THEN THERE IS POOR OPHELIA, WHO IS COMPARED TO A MERMAID IN THE ACCOUNT QUEEN GERTRUDE GIVES LAERTES OF THE FINAL MOMENTS OF HER LIFE, IN *HAMLET*, ACT IV.

'Her clothes spread wide,
And mermaid-like awhile
they bore her up,
Which time she chanted
snatches of old lauds,
As one incapable of her
own distress
Or like a creature
native and endued unto
that element.'

'On Jura's heath
how sweetly swell

THE MURMURS OF THE MOUNTAIN BEE!
HOW SOFTLY MOURNS THE WRITHED SHELL
OF JURA'S SHORE ITS PARENT SEA!

'But softer floating,
o'er the deep,

THE MERMAID'S SWEET SEA-SOOTHING LAY,
THAT CHARMED THE DANCING WAVES TO SLEEP
BEFORE THE BARK OF COLONSAY.'

– JOHN LEYDEN, SCOTTISH POET

147

Some parents of gender-non-conforming YOUNG PEOPLE IN THE UK CREATED AN ORGANIZATION CALLED

Mermaids

THAT OFFERS SUPPORT, COMMUNITY, AND MYRIAD RESOURCES FOR YOUNG PEOPLE AND THEIR FAMILIES.

One of Lady Gaga's
MANY PERSONAS IS A MERMAID NAMED

Yüyi,

WHO IS FEATURED IN HER VIDEO
FOR 'YOU AND I'.

Mermaid Spells

SOME BELIEVE THE GEMSTONE

aquamarine

– 'WATER OF THE SEA' – IS MADE FROM

the tears of mermaids.

(IN ANCIENT CHINESE FOLKLORE, MERMAID
TEARS TURN INTO PEARLS INSTEAD.)

Aquamarine

IS BELIEVED TO HAVE HEALING PROPERTIES,
*bringing calmness,
clarity, and courage*
TO THE WEARER.

154

Mermaid Spell for Finding Treasure

Mermaid spell for finding treasure

Set up an altar with shells and sea glass. Make a circle of smooth rocks and in the centre place a white candle. Light the candle and read these words from Anne Morrow Lindbergh's *Gift from the Sea* quietly to yourself.

'The sea does not reward those who are too anxious, too greedy, or too impatient. To dig for treasures shows not only impatience and greed, but lack of faith. Patience, patience, patience, is what the sea teaches. Patience and faith. One should lie empty, open, choiceless as a beach – waiting for a gift from the sea.'

Take five deep breaths, counting slowly to three as you inhale, holding the breath in for the count of two, and breathing out slowly to a count of three.

Now take three more breaths. Try to keep the same counting rhythm, but this time, instead of counting, breathe in thinking of the word 'faith' and breathe out thinking of the word 'empty'.

What gift will come to you today?

Close your eyes, not trying to force any thoughts, just letting yourself be open to whatever treasure awaits.

158

Mermaid Spell for Reconciling Your Duelling Nature

Mermaid spell for reconciling your duelling nature

Known for being brutal and beautiful, both protectors and destroyers of men, humanlike, but never quite part of our world, the one consistent trait that mermaids portray is inconsistency. As symbols of duality, they can help us embrace our likely less-dramatic contradictory aspects.

First, write a little in your journal or on a piece of paper about traits of your personality that tend to pull in opposite directions. Do you love parties but feel shy when speaking to new people? Live for sports but hate competition? Are you a morning person but get your best ideas late at night? Maybe some of these contradictions are bothersome – your love for minimalist spaces doesn't manifest itself in your perpetually messy desk – and maybe some make you feel quirky in a lovable way – you hate being the centre of attention but can't help breakdancing at every bar with a dance floor. Write down everything that comes to mind. When you're done, read over your list, trying not to judge one way or the other, simply observing yourself from a distance.

Now find yourself a quiet spot. (You don't need your list any more.) Sit near the ocean's edge if you can. If that's not possible, set yourself up with a few shells, a little bowl of salt water, and play some ocean sounds in the background.

 160

Think of syncing your breathing with the rhythm of the waves. In and out. Slowly. In and out. There is no rush. Let the rhythm repeat itself. Don't worry if you're not syncing exactly, the point is just to breathe deeply and become still within yourself as the tide goes in and out.

The ocean is dangerous but also life-giving. Beautiful but full of strange, alien-like creatures. Dark underneath but luminous in moonlight. A connection to worlds far away but a soothing reminder to be happy exactly where you are.

You, too, have many forces that pull in opposite directions – towards creation and destruction, towards darkness, and towards light. You needn't choose one side or the other, or give up conflicting traits. Like a mermaid, you're a shapeshifter. You're at home by the ocean.

Mermaid Spell for Finding Your Voice

Mermaid spell for finding your voice

Find a quiet place. Light a candle, burn some incense, and set up a little bowl of salt, which will help absorb negative energy. If you like, you could play some quiet music. Take a piece of paper, knowing you won't keep anything you write unless you want to. It is only for you. Answer the following questions:

In what settings are you comfortable expressing yourself? Are there settings in which you are not comfortable?

What forms do you like to use to express yourself? (Poetry, fashion, dance, social media posts.)

What are some disguises that you wear?

Do you feel there was a time in your life when you were more in touch with your essential self?

What changed?

What matters most to you?

Do you trust your instincts?

Now write whatever comes into your head first when you read the following sentence stems. Don't worry if what you say doesn't make sense or isn't the 'best' answer, just jot down the words as they come.

I am…
I feel…
The lesson I'm learning is…
I wish I could…

I'm looking for…
Home is…
My voice is…

Read back over what you've written. Pick three words that stand out to you and circle them. Now take a new piece of paper and write these three words in the centre. Soon you will close your eyes, think about those three words, and allow whatever associations they bring to come into your mind. Take a deep breath and close your eyes for a minute or two.

When you open your eyes, imagine you can hear a beautiful sound. It is someone singing. The melody is clear and light, coming to you from a faraway place, an enchanted place. You follow the sound and find that the singer is you.

When you feel ready, blow out the candle, dump out the salt, and rip up and recycle the paper (unless you want to keep it). The three words are a code that only you know.

166

Seaside Meditation

Seaside meditation

Find a spot by the sea, ideally, but you can always create your own mini 'beach retreat' with an ocean-scented candle, the sound of waves, and maybe some pictures from magazines of holidays at sea. What kind of sea feels the calmest to you? A tropical paradise? Then you'll want to imagine bright sun, palm trees, white sand, crystal-clear turquoise water. But maybe your idea of an afternoon spent by calming seas has colder, rougher water, a darker sky, and a cosy house where you can cuddle up and drink tea after coming home from a chilly walk along the rocky shore? Whatever scene speaks to you, try to imagine yourself in that place as you take a few deep breaths.

What are you looking at? Are you by the water? Are your feet in the sand? Or have you already gone home, taking a pocket full of sea glass with you?

As you breathe in, think of breathing calm into your body. As you breathe out, let any tension from the day go out, too. No one is asking anything from you right now. You are exactly where you need to be. You feel light. The sun and the salty air and the reassuring back-and-forth of the tide are with you.

Maybe there are some worrying thoughts coming into your head. That's okay. You don't have to chase them away; let them come in with the waves and go back out with the waves. You are steady.

Maybe you keep thinking of things you need to do. You'll get to them, but right now you are allowed to just be here, feeling yourself sink into the sand or the cosy couch with a nice blanket over you. The sea hasn't changed from the last time you came or the time before that. It is how you remember it to be and goes on as far as you can see. The day slows down by the sea. You can feel each minute. You're not rushing. You're not thinking about needing to answer anybody else or let anyone know what you're doing. You don't need to impress with a snapshot of what you see. The moment is here for you to treasure.

When you're ready, blow out the candle and say thank you to the sea for always being there for you.

Mermaid-Inspired Recipes

Sea foam milkshake

These days it seems you can order any possible combination of ingredients for smoothies. Mango, turmeric, pomegranate, coconut, chia seed, acai, ginger, parsley – and how about some flaxseeds for good measure? Superfoods are – well – super. But sometimes all these options can make your head spin. As you slow down long enough to hear mermaids sing from across the waves and ages, how about for a change trying a classic smoothie combo with ingredients you'll find at the nearest grocery store, no matter the season?

This healthy shake makes a great addition to breakfast or a midday pick-me-up. Although real sea foam is white (and tastes awful!) and the popular colour for coastal homes called 'sea foam' is close to aqua, this shake will probably be a less-attractive greenish colour. Don't worry! It's still nutritious and delicious. And as any mermaid who tried life on land will tell you, it's what's inside that counts.

Ingredients

2 BANANAS, ROUGHLY CHOPPED (FROZEN IS BEST, BUT YOU CAN ALWAYS ADD A LITTLE ICE IF YOU DON'T HAVE FROZEN ONES ON HAND)

500ML (17 ½FL OZ) ORANGE JUICE

500ML (17 ½FL OZ) WHOLE/FULL-FAT MILK

HANDFUL OF FRESH SPINACH, WASHED (SEE NOTE)

ORANGE SLICE, TO GARNISH

Method

1 Mix all the ingredients together in a blender until frothy so you can serve up a convincing glass of sea foam.

2 Pour into tumblers and garnish with a slice of orange.

Note: Try substituting kale or, if you're feeling really adventurous, rocket, beetroot greens, Swiss chard, or even pak choi. You can always add more greens, to your liking. And be sure to check your teeth in your hand mirror before heading out to sea!

Cucumber & seaweed salad

Prep Time: 10 minutes   Serves 4

Raw fish and a seaweed salad is a favourite mermaid meal. Let's skip the raw fish and make a tangy salad of cucumbers and seaweed instead. Bring along some bread, cheese, and fruit and you'll have a perfect summer picnic.

Ingredients

4 TBSP DRIED WAKAME SEAWEED

5 OR 6 CUCUMBERS

½ WHITE ONION

80ML (3FL OZ) RICE VINEGAR

2 TBSP SUGAR

FEW SHAKES OF SALT

1 TBSP SESAME SEEDS, TO SERVE

Method

1 Prepare your seaweed first by letting it soak in a bowl of water for 10 minutes.

2 Meanwhile, thinly slice the cucumbers and onion. Give all these ingredients a good squeeze to get out any excess water, then mix together in a serving bowl.

3 In a separate bowl, combine the vinegar and sugar.

4 Add the dressing to the salad and sprinkle on a little salt. Let the salad sit in the refrigerator for at least an hour. Serve with the sesame seeds scattered on top.

Crispy marine greens

Prep time: 10 minutes   Serves 4

Seaweed is full of vitamins and antioxidants, but if you're having a mermaid-inspired party and you want a little variety, you can always go with kale for a delicious, healthy snack. It's not a seaweed, although there is a perennial plant called sea kale, which also isn't a plant from the sea, but if it's good enough for The Mermaid Inn on Mermaid Street to serve, it's good enough for us. If you find yourself in the medieval town of Rye in East Sussex, England, and get a chance to swim in to The Mermaid Inn, don't miss the Giant's Fireplace Bar or the secret passageway. (If your interest in the paranormal extends to airborne creatures, you'll be intrigued by the inn's history of ghosts, too.)

Ingredients

2 BUNCHES OF GREEN KALE
2 TBSP OLIVE OIL
SEA SALT
BLACK PEPPER
1 TSP LEMON JUICE

OPTIONAL TOPPINGS – SESAME SEEDS, PARMESAN CHEESE, CUMIN, NUTRITIONAL YEAST, CURRY POWDER, CHILLI POWDER

Method

1 Remove the ends of the kale stems. Chop or tear apart the leaves and wash. Pat dry.

2 Drizzle the kale with oil and toss with sea salt and pepper. When the kale is fully coated, add one teaspoon of lemon juice. Add any of the optional toppings you'd like.

3 Spread out on a baking sheet (overlapping is fine) and put in a 200°C (400°F) oven for 10 minutes or so, until crispy, checking and stirring every few minutes. Keep an eye on the kale as it goes from looking raw to charred rather quickly. It won't taste good if it's burned.

4 Enjoy fresh!

Lemon zest sand dollar cookies

Prep time: 20 minutes (then allow the dough to chill overnight.)   Makes 18 cookies

Related to starfish, and also called sea cookies, sand dollars are lovely sea urchins, but they are best left undisturbed or should be returned to water if they are found outside it. (In many places it's illegal to take live sand dollars.) These cookies look like the sea creatures; they go great with a cup of tea in the afternoon (or even the morning) and aren't overly sweet. The lemon zest adds a nice zing. Those who want to avoid nuts can use a knife to make the sand dollar pattern before baking.

Ingredients

110G (4OZ) BUTTER, SOFTENED
150G (5OZ) BROWN SUGAR
1 EGG
2 TBSP WHOLE/FULL-FAT MILK
1 TSP VANILLA EXTRACT
130G (4 ½OZ) PLAIN FLOUR

1 TSP BICARBONATE OF SODA
½ TSP BAKING POWDER
½ TSP SALT
GRATED ZEST OF 1 LEMON
SLICED ALMONDS (90 SLICES)

Method

1 Preheat the oven to 180°C (350°F).

2 Cream the butter and sugar together. Separately, beat the egg with the milk and vanilla. When the butter and sugar are fully mixed, combine with the egg mixture.

3 In a separate bowl, mix the flour, bicarbonate of soda, baking powder, and salt. Combine with the wet ingredients and add the lemon zest. If the dough is dry, add a bit more milk. Leave the dough to chill in the fridge overnight to keep the dough from spreading as it bakes.

4 Shape into small balls and space them 5cm (2 inches) apart on a greased baking sheet. Use a cup dipped in powdered sugar/icing sugar to flatten out the balls and place five sliced almonds on each cookie in a star shape.

5 Cook in the oven until golden brown on top – about 10 minutes. Enjoy!

Shipwreck island pancakes

Prep time: 20 minutes
Makes 4 big pancakes, or 8 smaller ones

You've had blueberry, banana, maybe even chocolate chips. You've added maple syrup, of course, agave syrup on good days, and whipped cream when it's your birthday, or your friend's birthday, or the birthday of someone you once met somewhere. But have you tried a tropic-inspired version of your favourite Saturday morning treat? If you're actually shipwrecked on an island or experienced at being self-sufficient, you can begin this recipe by whacking a whole coconut against a pointy rock to get it open (please only choose this method if you have serious DIY credentials, not one afternoon spent repurposing a milk carton into a bird feeder). For the rest of us, pre-shredded coconut will do. Hey, you're making pancakes from scratch while your friends queue for outrageously priced and absurdly overcustomized coffee creations. Before you get frustrated when you accidentally set off your smoke alarm, remember the law of pancake-making – the first few never come out right. They're either overcooked or undercooked or too crumbly or too thick or too brown or too pale. Those are the ones you eat yourself (maybe not the undercooked ones) before you call anyone else to the table.

Ingredients

75G (2 ¾OZ) PLAIN FLOUR

1 TSP BAKING POWDER

2 SHAKES OF SALT

1 EGG

175ML (6FL OZ) WHOLE/FULL-FAT MILK

1 TSP APPLE SAUCE

1 TSP LIME JUICE

1 TBSP COCONUT FLAKES

BUTTER, FOR FRYING

To serve

MAPLE SYRUP

BUTTER

LIME SLICES

Method

1 Mix the flour, baking powder, and salt together in a large bowl. In a separate bowl, beat the egg then add the milk, apple sauce, and lime juice. Pour the wet ingredients into the dry and stir to combine – try not to overmix – then leave for 10 minutes. Stir in the coconut flakes.

2 Melt a pat of butter on a large, flat skillet/frying pan and test the temperature with a small bit of pancake batter to be sure you have the heat right. Pancakes are a bit finicky – too hot or too cold (and therefore cooking too long) and they won't come out right. They'll be edible, and if you're truly shipwrecked, probably more than serviceable, but aim for the Goldilocks' 'just-right' temperature. Ladle the batter into the pan and flip when you see bubbles. As far as the size and shape go, the more imperfect the better, as you'll get more intriguing 'island' shapes. So don't worry about turning the pan to get nice, round pancakes.

3 Serve with maple syrup, or even just butter, and garnish with lime slices.

Sea-swirl fudge

Prep time: 15 minutes, plus 2 hours to chill
Makes 28 pieces

Fudge is great any time of the year, but this mint and sea-salt version makes a particularly delicious Christmas treat for friends and neighbours. For variation, and a little protein, and as long as no one has a nut-allergy, you can always add chopped walnuts before you pour the mixture into the pan. Don't let anyone know how easy the recipe is! Let them think you swam all day collecting pure salt from the sea.

Ingredients

400G (14OZ) CAN SWEETENED CONDENSED MILK

525G (18 ½OZ) PLAIN CHOCOLATE CHIPS

2 TBSP BUTTER

1 TSP VANILLA EXTRACT

175G (6OZ) MINT CHOCOLATE CHIPS

GENEROUS HANDFUL OF GOOD-QUALITY SEA SALT (IF YOU'RE IN THE MOOD FOR A TREASURE HUNT, SEL DE GUÉRANDE FROM BRITTANY, FRANCE, IS OUT OF THIS WORLD)

COCONUT OIL, FOR GREASING

Method

1 Grease a 20 × 20cm (8 × 8 inch) baking tin, including the sides. In a saucepan set over a pan of gently simmering water, stirring occasionally, heat (or microwave) the condensed milk, plain chocolate chips, butter, and vanilla, being sure not to scald it. When thoroughly combined and easy to stir, pour into the tin and sprinkle with sea salt.

2 Separately, melt the mint chocolate chips in a bowl set over a pan of gently simmering water (or in the microwave), stirring occasionally. Once melted, drizzle this over the top of your fudge for a swirly effect.

3 Refrigerate for 2 hours, then once set, cut into bite-size pieces and enjoy in the dark, winter months inside, as you dream of a holiday at sea.

Mermaid Crafts & Activities

Mermaid crown

Looking for a simple craft project or great gift idea? Look no further, mermaid crowns are here! Just follow these simple steps to handcraft your own must-have accessory fit for a mermaid princess. Add your own spin with glitter, sequins – or any bits of mermaid magic you like. Your imagination is the limit!

Materials

GREEN, TURQUOISE, AND SILVER FELT
    (OR ANY COLOURS OF YOUR CHOOSING)

SEQUINS, PEARL BEADS, RHINESTONES,
    RIBBONS, OR ANY OTHER DECORATIONS
    YOU CHOOSE

PLASTIC HEADBAND

Equipment

SCISSORS

FABRIC MARKERS (SLIGHTLY
    DARKER SHADES THAN YOUR
    CHOSEN FELT COLOURS)

CRAFT GLUE OR A HOT
    GLUE-GUN

Method

1 Start by cutting out felt shapes to decorate your crown – cut out as many decorations as you want according to how lush you want your mermaid crown to be. We suggest 2 large seaweed leaves, 5 medium, 2 small, 2 large, and 2 small seashells, and 1 large and 2 small starfish.

2 Add detail to your decorations using the fabric markers, by shading or drawing onto your shapes. Glue on sequins or other decorations for added sparkle and interest.

3 Glue the cut-out pieces to the headband. We suggest starting with the seaweed leaves, then the biggest shapes first, followed by the medium and smaller ones on top, radiating out from the centre. Glue the bigger seashells and starfish in a cluster in the centre, with the smaller ones either side. Experiment to find an arrangement you like.

4 Embellish your crown by gluing on different-sized pearl beads, rhinestones, or any other mermaid glitter you like for extra mermaid sparkle.

Seaside bath scrub

Makes enough to fill a small mason jar

Swimming is one of the best forms of exercise you can do, but after a long day of kicking up your fin, your muscles may be a little sore. When you come home, treat yourself to a luxurious sea-inspired bath scrub. If you're using the scrub right away, you don't necessarily need to colour it, but if you're giving it as a gift, it looks lovely to pack some blue salts in a little jar and add a ribbon. Either way, store in a jar with a tight-fitting lid.

Please note: while lavender essential oil is deemed safe for use, pregnant or lactating women, or individuals with allergies or sensitivities, should consult a medical professional before using essential oils.

With thanks to the lovely Jessica Luk, whose enchanted home-made bath scrubs inspired this recipe.

Ingredients

135G (4 ½OZ) HIMALAYAN SEA SALT (IF YOU DON'T HAVE IT, THE SAME AMOUNT OF TABLE SALT WILL DO)

1 TSP BICARBONATE OF SODA

100G (3 ½OZ) SUGAR

125ML (4 ¼FL OZ) OIL (OLIVE OR COCONUT)

5–8 DROPS LAVENDER OIL (OR 1 TBSP VANILLA EXTRACT)

3 DROPS BLUE FOOD COLOURING (OPTIONAL)

188

Method

1 Mix the salt, bicarbonate of soda, and sugar together. Pour in the olive or coconut oil and mix.

2 Add the drops of lavender oil or vanilla extract. When fully mixed, add the blue food colouring, if you like. (If you're feeling super adventurous, you can make blue food colouring from red cabbage, see below.)

3 Run a bath, then step in, lean back, remember your day at sea, and scrub your skin for a lovely, natural exfoliated feeling.

All-natural blue food colouring

If you'd rather use all-natural colouring, and you are feeling particularly adventurous, trying boiling 1 chopped red cabbage in 2 litres (70fl oz) of water, then scoop out the cabbage and reduce the cooking water to about a third, adding bicarbonate of soda until you achieve the blue colour of your sea dreams. Meanwhile, sauté the cabbage with some oil, finely sliced onion, garlic, red wine, and a little brown sugar for a delicious treat.

Trinket holder

If you're a collector of sea glass, shells, and other shiny trinkets, you'll need somewhere special to keep them – especially the tiny ones. This shell jewellery holder will make the perfect place. Decorate it in whatever colour you wish – pale pink for sand with some silver glitter makes for a particularly delicate and fairytale-inspired palette, but perhaps you'd rather stick with a variety of blue hues for the sea.

Materials

LIGHT-COLOURED SCALLOP SHELL, PREFERABLY WITHOUT ANY BREAKS

PAINTBRUSH

PRIMER (OPTIONAL)

ACRYLIC PAINT IN YOUR PREFERRED COLOUR

SILVER GLITTER GLUE

Method

1. Clean the shell, removing any sand or debris. Decide how you'll paint it. Different colours on the inside and outside? A pattern? A design? To start, you might want to keep things simple, opting for one or two solid colours.

2. If you're using primer, paint a single coat. Let it dry and repeat, being sure to let the shell dry before applying the paint.

3. Wet your brush. Add a tiny bit of water to your paint and have a go at decorating your shell. When the paint dries, add a row of silver glitter along the outer rim of the inside of the shell and leave to dry.

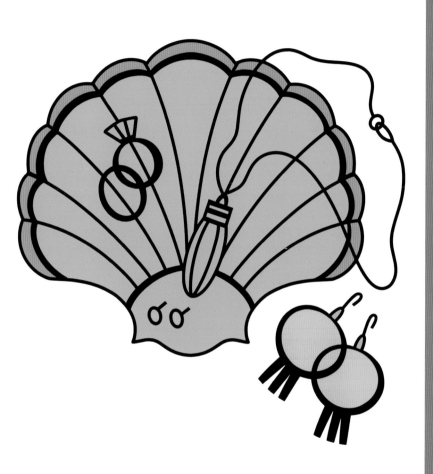

Beach mandala

'Mandala' means circle in Sanskrit. The sea bringeth and the sea taketh away.

The best time to find treasures from the ocean is right before or after low tide during a new or full moon. A storm brings an abundance of sea treasure, but wait until you're sure it's over before you set out on the hunt.

It's lovely to make keepsakes from the treasures you collect; you'll want to keep some of your creations, and give others away, but it's also fun to make a gift for someone else. Beach mandalas are a wonderful way to spend time by the sea and celebrate the fleeting beauty of your creation – there is something uniquely satisfying about making a piece of art that you know you cannot keep. Like sandcastles, it reminds you to be in the moment, enjoying what you have without always needing to hold on to it. Surely our favourite oceanic shapeshifters would approve?

Method

1. Consult the phases of the moon and the tidal calendar to pick the best time for beach-combing.

2. Don't limit yourself to only shells and sea glass. Rocks, sticks, seaweed, leaves, petals – all of these will be quite lovely in your mandala. Try to find ones that are loose (rather than, say, picking petals from a flower).

3 Spread out your haul on a towel and examine it. Do you want to group like with like? Or perhaps follow a pattern instead, rotating through different items as you might beads on a necklace? Take your inspiration from the Fibonacci spirals found in conch and snail shells (as well as many other places in nature, from pinecones to spiral galaxies). Start in the centre and circle outward in ever-wider arches on the sand.

4 While you're working, try to relax. Part of the joy of mandalas is in the quiet, contemplative focus of making them.

5 Stand back and admire your work. Take a picture, if you like, or else just allow yourself to enjoy the ephemeral artwork.

UNICORNS are REAL, the mermaids TOLD ME

— ANONYMOUS

Mermaid Inspiration

*M*ermaid love has inspired poetry, motivated women seeking access to the primal feminine, entertained crowds, and even inspired a company that makes hand-sewn tails. Although throughout their several-thousand-year history mermaids have also been known to be dangerously seductive, marvellously protective harbingers of doom, and at times intent on revenge. In contrast, today's mermaids tend to be whimsical, appealing to our longing for a world where we can swim to the rhythm of our own fins.

'Nobody has the right to lure your

voice

out of you.'

— *THE MERMAID'S VOICE RETURNS IN THIS ONE*, AMANDA LOVELACE (2019)

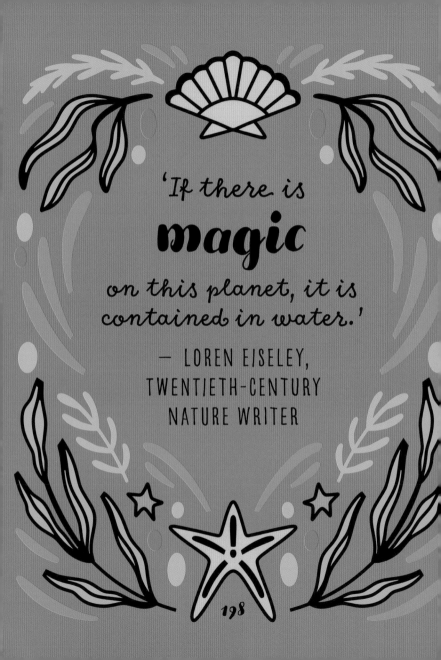

'If there is

magic

on this planet, it is
contained in water.'

— LOREN EISELEY,
TWENTIETH-CENTURY
NATURE WRITER

'I ADDRESS YOU ALL TONIGHT FOR WHO YOU *truly* ARE: *wizards, mermaids, travellers, adventurers, and magicians.* YOU ARE THE *true, dreamers.'*

— *THE INVENTION OF HUGO CABRET,*
BRIAN SELZNICK (2007)

Mermen –

REMEMBER, YOU CAN CHANNEL YOUR
inner mermaid, too.
SHELLS, GLITTER, GLIMMER,
SEQUINS, SEA GLASS –
*all the treasures
of the deep are yours.*

'Many nights she stood by the open window, LOOKING UP THROUGH THE DARK BLUE WATER, AND WATCHING THE FISH AS THEY SPLASHED ABOUT WITH THEIR FINS AND TAILS. SHE COULD SEE THE

moon and stars

SHINING FAINTLY; BUT THROUGH THE WATER THEY LOOKED LARGER THAN THEY DO TO OUR EYES. WHEN SOMETHING LIKE A BLACK CLOUD PASSED BETWEEN HER AND THEM, SHE KNEW THAT IT WAS

EITHER A WHALE SWIMMING OVER
HER HEAD, OR A SHIP FULL OF HUMAN
BEINGS, WHO NEVER IMAGINED THAT
a pretty little mermaid
WAS STANDING BENEATH THEM,
*holding out her white
hands towards the keel
of their ship.'
— *THE LITTLE MERMAID,*
HANS CHRISTIAN ANDERSEN

10 ways to help protect mermaids

1 STOP BUYING PLASTIC WATER BOTTLES. THERE ARE MANY COLOURFUL, SLEEK, REUSABLE WATER BOTTLES AVAILABLE. FILL YOURS UP WITH NICE COLD WATER AND CARRY IT WITH YOU.

2 REDUCE YOUR CARBON FOOTPRINT. WALK OR TAKE PUBLIC TRANSPORT WHENEVER POSSIBLE.

3 BEFORE YOU VOTE, TAKE TIME TO LOOK AT POLITICIANS' VIEWS ON CLIMATE CHANGE.

4 ORGANIZE A 'CLEAN THE BEACH' DAY. BRING COFFEE AND DOUGHNUTS (OR MAYBE SAND DOLLAR COOKIES! (SEE P. 178))

5 BUY SEAFOOD THAT IS HARVESTED IN SUSTAINABLE WAYS.

6 BRING CLOTH SHOPPING BAGS WITH YOU TO THE GROCERY STORE.

7 DONATE TO GROUPS DEDICATED TO REDUCING CLIMATE CHANGE AND MARINE CONSERVATION.

8 EAT LESS MEAT. (LOOK UP MEATLESS MONDAY ONLINE FOR INSPIRATION.)

9 TRANSFER INVESTMENTS FROM FOSSIL FUELS TO RENEWABLE ENERGY.

10 TALK TO YOUR FRIENDS ABOUT THE IMPORTANCE OF PROTECTING OUR OCEANS.

Lessons from mermaids

1 LIFE IS FULL OF POSSIBILITIES. DON'T BE AFRAID OF CHANGE.

2 NEVER MISS A CHANCE TO TAKE A BREAK IN A SUNNY SPOT.

3 STRONG CURRENTS BUILD RESILIENCE.

4 THINK OUTSIDE YOUR FINS.

5 SING.

6 HOLD FAST TO YOUR DREAMS, NO MATTER HOW UNREALISTIC OTHERS THINK THEY ARE.

7   BE ON THE LOOKOUT FOR HIDDEN TREASURE.

8   EMBRACE COMPLEXITY.

9   MAKE FRIENDS WITH SMALL CREATURES SWIMMING BESIDE YOU.

10 YOUR VOICE IS YOURS; DON'T LET ANYBODY TAKE IT FROM YOU.

11 DON'T BE AFRAID TO TRY ON A NEW ROLE, BUT DON'T HIDE WHO YOU REALLY ARE.

'Thou rememberest
Since once I sat upon
a promontory
And heard a mermaid on
a dolphin's back
Uttering such dulcet and
harmonious breath
That the rude sea grew
civil at her song
And certain stars shot
madly from their spheres
To hear the seamaid's music?'

— OBERON IN *A MIDSUMMER
NIGHT'S DREAM*, ACT II, SCENE 1,
WILLIAM SHAKESPEARE

'I must be a
mermaid, Rango.
I HAVE NO FEAR OF DEPTHS AND A GREAT
fear of shallow living.'
— THE FOUR-CHAMBERED HEART,
ANAÏS NIN

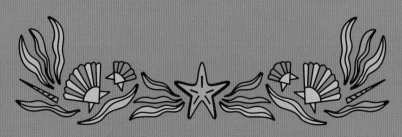

'She would be half a
planet away,
FLOATING IN A TURQUOISE SEA,
dancing by the
moonlight.'

— *WHITE OLEANDER, JANET FITCH*

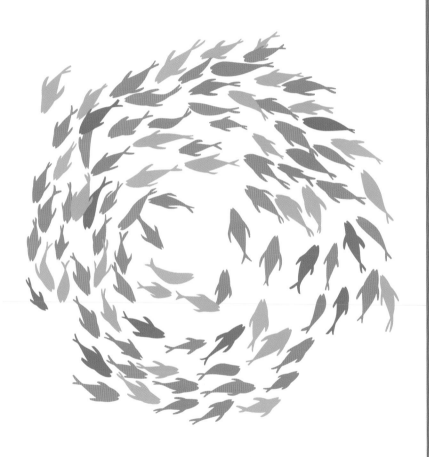

Bibliography

American Museum of Natural History staff; 'Becoming Mermaids', part of the Mythic Creatures exhibition, American Museum of Natural History; www.amnh.org/exhibitions/mythic-creatures/water/becoming-mermaids (accessed 20 March 2019)

American Social History Project; 'The FeeJee Mermaid Exhibit', The Lost Museum Archive; online at https://lostmuseum.cuny.edu/archive/exhibit/mermaid (accessed 5 April 2019)

Angry Mermaid Award; online at www.angrymermaid.org/

Ashton, John. *Curious Creatures in Zoology: With 130 Illustrations Throughout the Text*. John C. Nimmo (London, 1890)

Banse, Karl. 'Mermaids – Their Biology, Culture, and Demise.' *Limnology and Oceanography*, vol. 35, no. 1, 1990, pp. 148–153. JSTOR; www.jstor.org/stable/2837348 (accessed 24 April 2019)

BBC News; 'Little Mermaid: Copenhagen statue a target for vandals', BBC News, June 15, 2017; online at www.bbc.com/news/world-europe-40293396 (accessed 17 April 2019)

Carmichael, Alexander. *Carmina Gadelica: Hymns and Incantations*. Floris Books. (Edinburgh, 1994)

Cipriani, Casey. 'How Ariel In *The Little Mermaid* Led To Far More Feminist Princesses Like Mulan & Merida, According To Voice Actor Jodi Benson'. Bustle; online at www.bustle.com/p/how-ariel-in-the-little-mermaid-led-to-far-more-feminist-princesses-like-mulan-merida-according-to-voice-actor-jodi-benson-15942919 (accessed 23 April 2019)

Cormier, Roger. '15 Surprising Facts about Splash.' Mental Floss; online at http://mentalfloss.com/article/76738/15-surprising-facts-about-splash (accessed 3 April 2019)

Costantino, Grace. 'The Beautiful Monster: Mermaids.' 31 October 2014; Biodiversity Heritage Library; Blog Web, 28 March 2019.

De Vos, Lauren and Salinas de León, Pelayo. 'Feeling the Heat.' *Save Our Seas* magazine, December 2018; online at www.saveourseasmagazine.com/feeling-the-heat/ (accessed 1 May 2019)

Elbein, Asher. 'Sirens of Greek Myth Were Bird-Women, Not Mermaids.' Audobon 6 April 2018. Online at https://www.audubon.org/news/sirens-greek-myth-were-bird-women-not-mermaids

Guitton, Matthieu, J. ed. *Mermaids.* Intellect Books (Chicago, 2016)

Hall, Manly P. and Augustus Knapp, J. *The Secret Teachings of all the Ages, An Encyclopedic Outline of Masonic, Hermetic, Qabbalistic and Rosicrucian Symbolical Philosophy.* H.S. Corcker Company, Inc. (San Francisco, 1928)

History staff. 'Columbus mistakes manatees for mermaids.' This Day in History, 24 November 2009. A&E Television Networks.

Hongrui, Li. 'Mermaids in Chinese fairy tales.' *China Daily*, February 2016; online at http://www.chinadaily.com.cn/culture/2016-02/22/content_23591906.htm (accessed 7 April 2019)

Horspool, Susette. 'Real Mermaid Life in the Ocean.' Exemplore, September 2017; online at exemplore.com/cryptids/Real-Mermaid-Life-in-the-Ocean (accessed 8 April 2019)

Jagernauth, Kevin. 'Producer Brian Grazer Says He's Remaking *Splash* But With a Twist'. 6 June 2016; online at https://theplaylist.net/producer-brian-grazer-says-hes-remaking-splash-twist-20160606/ (accessed 14 April 2019)

Jerome, Jim. 'A Whale of a Tale.' *People Weekly*, 9 April 1984

Kanai, Lang. 'How Did Manatees Inspire Mermaid Legends?' *National Geographic*, 25 November 2014.

Kellermann, Annette. 'Diving into a Crocodile Pit'. National Film and Sound Archive of Australia Oral Histories, 1974; online at www.nfsa.gov.au/collection/curated/diving-crocodile-pit-annette-kellerman (accessed 18 April 2019)

Kingshill, Sophia. *Mermaids*. UK Little Toller Books (Dorset, 2015)

Love, Jessica. *Julián is a Mermaid*. Candlewick (Somerville, 2018)

Lovelace, Amanda. *the mermaid's voice returns in this one*. Andrew McMeel (Kansas City, 2019)

'Mermaid'. *The Oxford Companion to the Body*. Encyclopedia.com. 24 April 2019; www.encyclopedia.com (accessed 14 April 2019)

Mermaids; online at www.mermaidsuk.org.uk/

Oliver, Narelle. *Mermaids Most Amazing*. G.P. Putnam's Sons (New York, 2001)

Phillpotts, Beatrice. *Mermaids*. Ballantine Books (New York, 1980)

Pliny the Elder, *Natural History*, Philemon Hollands translation, 1601

Radsken, Jill. 'Feejee Mermaid is unattractive attraction.' *The Harvard Gazette*, October 2017; online at https://news.harvard.edu/gazette/story/2017/10/feejee-mermaid-offers-haunting-tale-at-harvard-museum/ (accessed 30 April 2017)

Ray, Jane. *The Little Mermaid and Other Fishy Tales*. Boxer Books (New York, 2014)

Roberts, Kayleigh. 'We asked a marine biologist to solve the mystery of how mermaids have sex.' Hello Giggles, February 2016; online at https://hellogiggles.com/lifestyle/mermaid-sex/ (Web, 30 April 2019)

Ross, David, ed. 'Zennor Church and the Mermaid of Zennor.' Britain Express; online at www.britainexpress.com/counties/cornwall/churches/zennor.htm (accessed 14 April 2019)

Russell, W.M.S., and Russell, F.S. 'The Origin of the Sea Bishop.' *Folklore* Vol. 86, No. 2 (Summer, 1975), pp. 94–98

Smithsonian National Museum of African Art staff. 'Mami Wata': Arts for Water spirits in Africa and Its Diasporas, Smithsonian National Museum of African Art; online at https://africa.si.edu/exhibits/mamiwata/intro.html (accessed 14 April 2019)

Sparks, Amber. 'The Original *Little Mermaid*.' *The Paris Review*, 16 March 2018.

Thorne, Russ. *The Magical History of Mermaids*. Flame Tree Publishing (London, 2018)

Turgeon, Carolyn. *The Mermaid Handbook: An Alluring Treasury of Literature, Lore, Art, Recipes, and Projects*. HarperCollins (London, 2018)

Young, Lauren. 'In 1562 Map-Makers Thought America Was Full of Mermaids, Giants, and Dragons.' *Atlas Obscura*, December 2016; online at https://blogs.loc.gov/folklife/2018/05/the-mermaid/ (accessed 14 April 2019)

Waugh, Arthur. 'The Folklore of the Merfolk.' *Folklore*, vol. 71, no. 2, 1960, pp. 73–84. JSTOR; online at www.jstor.org/stable/1258382

Weeki Wachee Springs State Park, staff. 'The Magnificent History of Weeki Wachee Springs State Park.' Weeki Wachee Springs State Park; online at https://weekiwachee.com/about-us/ (accessed 8 April 2019)

Wessing, Robert. 'A Princess from Sunda: Some Aspects of Nyai Roro Kidul.' *Asian Folklore Studies*, vol. 56, no. 2, 1997, pp. 317–353. JSTOR; online at www.jstor.org/stable/1178730.

Whitfield, Anna. 'Mermaid tales appear in myths around the world – Arnhem Land included.' ABC News Australia; online at www.abc.net.au/news/2018-06-11/mermaids-across-the-world-arnhem-land/9846210 (accessed 14 April 2019)

Winick, Stephen. '"The Mermaid": the Fascinating Tail Behind an Ancient Ballad.' *Folklife Today*: American Folklife Center & Veterans History project. 24 May 2018. (Web, 3 April 2019). Online at https://blogs.loc.gov/folklife/2018/05/the-mermaid/

World Book Encyclopedia, World Book (Chicago, 2019), p. 475

Acknowledgements

Thanks to Caitlin who conceived of the idea for this book and lent it many mer-tastic ideas, along with great queries and edits, as always. Thanks are due to Sugar Bear for her input as well – plus she once rescued a falling man, surely earning the approval of protective mermaids everywhere, along with a nickname that has stayed, now for over a decade. Thanks to my mom and aunt Ellen, too – Celtic sea-maidens who taught me to love the ocean and spent many a summer (and winter) afternoon with me, combing the treasures of Laurel Beach. Laura Korzon – I haven't met you, but I'm grateful for the chance to lose myself in the imaginary realms you conjure. Whatever charm the book offers will be largely due to your work. Jacqui Caulton, thank you as ever for your beautiful aquatic design and boundless creativity. Thank you also to the wonderful editorial team of Helena Caldon, Rachel Malig, Carron Brown, and Lucy Kingett. Petra's mermaid stories have enchanted me, and Wally has helped with several related efforts – including late-night recipe development.

About the author & illustrator

Rachel Federman is a writer, musician, and non-profit consultant who has written over twenty books for adults and children, including *The Mindful Gardener* (Clarkson Potter, 2017) and *Test Your Dog's IQ* (HarperCollins, 2016). She once saw three mermaids in the fountain at Washington Square Park in New York City. No one seemed to know how they got there.

Laura Korzon is an artist, illustrator, and designer, born and raised in Lancaster, Pennsylvania, USA. She graduated from Rhode Island School of Design in 2010 and spends her days creating colourful graphics for cards, stationery, clothing, and books, including *Unicornucopia* (HarperCollins, 2018).

223